Writing
Learning Stations
Grades 6–8
English Language Arts series

Authors: Schyrlet Cameron and Suzanne Myers

Editors: Mary Dieterich and Sarah M. Anderson

Proofreader: Margaret Brown

COPYRIGHT © 2013 Mark Twain Media, Inc.

ISBN 978-1-62223-005-1

Printing No. CD-404180

Mark Twain Media, Inc., Publishers
Distributed by Carson-Dellosa Publishing LLC

Visit us at www.carsondellosa.com

Table of Contents

To the Teacher...1
Common Core State Standards Matrix......2

Unit: Fact and Opinion
Teacher Page 3
Activities
Station One: *Writing Opinion
     Statements*..4
Station Two: *Writing Fact and Opinion
     Statements*..5
Station Three: *Fact and Opinion in
     Advertising*..6
Station Four: *Editorials*..........................7
Station Five: *Recognizing Facts*..............8
Station Six: *Write a Letter to the Editor*....9
Handout
Comparing Advertisements....................10

Unit: Narrative Techniques: Dialogue
Teacher Page 11
Activities
Station One: *Proofreading Dialogue*.......12
Station Two: *Punctuating Dialogue*.........13
Station Three: *Writing Conversation*.......14
Station Four: *Analyzing Dialogue*...........15
Handouts
Proofreading Symbols...........................16
Guidelines for Writing Dialogue.............17

Unit: Editing and Proofreading
Teacher Page 18
Activities
Station One: *Proofreading a Business
     Letter*..19
Station Two: *Punctuation, Capitalization,
     and Grammar*...................................20
Station Three: *Editing for Clarity, Transition,
     and Order*...21
Station Four: *Proofreading Scavenger
     Hunt*...22

Unit: Analyzing and Drawing Evidence From Informational Text
Teacher Page 23
Activities
Details! Details! Details! 24
Station One: *Textile Mill Workers:
     Photograph A*...................................25
Station Two: *Textile Mill Workers:
     Photograph B*...................................26
Station Three: *Textile Mill Workers:
     Photograph C*...................................27
Station Four: *Textile Mill Workers:
     Photograph D*...................................28
Station Five: *Textile Mill Workers:
     Photograph E*...................................29
Station Six: *Textile Mill Workers:
     Photograph F*...................................30
Reflection: Textile Mill Workers..............31

Unit: Analyzing and Drawing Evidence From Literature
Teacher Page 32
Activities
Station One: *Character Traits* 33
Station Two: *Flat or Round Characters*...34
Station Three: *Static and Dynamic
     Characters* 35
Station Four: *Story Map* 36
     Protagonist or Antagonist 37
Station Five: *Three Little Pigs: Story
     and Poem*...38
*Reflection: Traditional Versus Modern
     Variations*...39
Handouts
*The Three Little Pigs
     (Traditional Version)* 40
Examples of Character Traits 42
Teacher Resource Page
*The Three Little Pigs
     (Modern Variations)* 43

Answer Keys 44

To the Teacher

In the *English Language Arts* (ELA) *series*, students in grades six through eight explore reading, writing, and language in a learning station environment. Learning stations engage students in individual or small group activities. Learning stations are an instructional strategy that can be used to target specific skills.

Each book in the ELA series features five or six units of study. Each unit has a teacher page that identifies the goal, states the standards, lists materials and setup for the activities, and provides instructions to be presented to students. Also, there are questions for opening discussion and student reflection. (Note: It is important for the teacher to introduce, model, or review the concepts or skills with the students at the beginning of each unit.)

Books in the ELA Series

- *Reading: Literature Learning Stations, Grades 6–8*
  The units focus on alliteration, rhyme, plot and setting, tone and mood, and poetry.

- *Reading: Informational Text Learning Stations, Grades 6–8*
  The units focus on citing evidence, bias, point of view, propaganda techniques, organizational text structures, and text features.

- *Writing Learning Stations, Grades 6–8*
  The units focus on fact and opinion, characterization, making inferences, proofreading, and dialogue.

- *Language Learning Stations, Grades 6–8*
  The units focus on punctuation, dictionary usage, figurative language, roots and affixes, and word meaning.

Writing Learning Stations, Grades 6–8, contains five units of study. Each unit consists of four to six learning station activities. The activity at each station is designed to create interest, provide practice, and stimulate discussion. These units will help students become better writers as they learn how to express their opinions and back them up with evidence, make inferences from photos and literature, analyze characters in literature, write dialogue, and develop good proofreading and editing skills. Whenever applicable, media/technology and speaking/listening skills are integrated into the activity. Handouts are provided as supplemental resources.

The units of study in the ELA series are meant to supplement or enhance the regular classroom English Language Arts curriculum. The station activities are correlated to the strands of the English Language Arts Common Core State Standards.

Common Core State Standards Matrix

English Language Arts Standards: Writing

Units of Study	Grade Level																													
	W.6.1	W.6.2	W.6.3	W.6.4	W.6.5	W.6.6	W.6.7	W.6.8	W.6.9	W.6.10	W.7.1	W.7.2	W.7.3	W.7.4	W.7.5	W.7.6	W.7.7	W.7.8	W.7.9	W.7.10	W.8.1	W.8.2	W.8.3	W.8.4	W.8.5	W.8.6	W.8.7	W.8.8	W.8.9	W.8.10
Fact and Opinion	X										X										X									
Narrative Techniques: Dialogue			X										X										X							
Editing and Proofreading					X										X										X					
Analyzing and Drawing Evidence From Informational Text									X										X										X	
Analyzing and Drawing Evidence From Literature									X										X										X	

Teacher Page

Unit: Fact and Opinion

Goal: Students will be able to distinguish fact from opinion in expository text.

Common Core State Standards (CCSS):

6th Grade	7th Grade	8th Grade
W.6.1. Write arguments to support claims with clear reasons and relevant evidence.	W.7.1. Write arguments to support claims with clear reasons and relevant evidence.	W.8.1. Write arguments to support claims with clear reasons and relevant evidence.

© Copyright 2010. National Governors Association Center for Best Practices and Council of Chief State School Officers. All rights reserved.

Materials List/Setup

Station 1: Writing Opinion Statements (Activity)
Station 2: Writing Fact and Opinion Statements (Activity)
Station 3: Fact and Opinion in Advertising (Activity); Comparing Advertisements (Handout)
Station 4: Editorials (Activity); a selection of newspaper editorials
Station 5: Recognizing Facts (Activity); a selection of newspapers
Station 6: Write a Letter to the Editor (Activity)

Activity: one copy per student
Handout: one copy per each student in a group

Opening: Discussion Questions (Teacher-Directed)

1. What is a fact?
2. How do you know something is a fact?
3. What is an opinion?
4. What are the signal words that can help you identify opinion statements?

Student Instructions for Learning Stations

At the learning stations, you will examine, analyze, and write fact and opinion statements. Discuss your answers with other team members after completing each activity.

Closure: Reflection

The following question can be used to stimulate discussion or as a journaling activity.

1. Why is it important to be able to determine the difference between fact and opinion?

Name: _____ Date: _____

Station One: Writing Opinion Statements

Directions: Take a fact and rewrite it as an opinion. Remember, opinion statements sometimes contain signal words such as *best, most,* or *probably.* Opinion statements may also contain phrases such as *I believe, I think,* or *I feel.*

    Example (FACT):   Friday is the last day of the school week.

    Example (OPINION):   Friday is the best day of the week.

Fact	Opinion
Mount St. Helens erupted in 1980.	
Grover Cleveland was the only president to be married in the White House.	
Venus and Uranus are the only two planets that rotate clockwise.	
George Washington Carver developed approximately 300 uses for the peanut.	
The colors in a rainbow are red, orange, yellow, green, blue, indigo, and violet.	
During the American Revolutionary War, each state printed its own paper money.	

Name: _____ Date: _____

Station Two: Writing Fact and Opinion Statements

A **fact** is something that can be proven true with some form of evidence. An **opinion** expresses what a person or group thinks, feels, or believes.

Directions: Write one fact and one opinion statement for each topic.

Example Topic: Nile River

Example Fact: The Nile is the longest river in the world.

Example Opinion: A boat trip on the Nile River is a once-in-a-lifetime adventure.

1. Topic: Cell Phones

    Fact: _____

    Opinion: _____

2. Topic: Texting

    Fact: _____

    Opinion: _____

3. Topic: School Uniforms

    Fact: _____

    Opinion: _____

4. Topic: Year-Round School

    Fact: _____

    Opinion: _____

5. Topic: Smoking

    Fact: _____

    Opinion: _____

Name: _____ Date: _____

Station Three: Fact and Opinion in Advertising

Directions: Examine the two advertisements on the Comparing Advertisements handout. Fill in the graphic organizer with fact and opinion statements found on each advertisement.

	Advertisement #1	Advertisement #2
Claim		
Facts		
Opinions		

1. Advertisement #1: Do the facts support the claim? Explain your answer.

    _____

    _____

    _____

2. Advertisement #2: Do the facts support the claim? Explain your answer.

    _____

    _____

    _____

Name: _____ Date: _____

Station Four: Editorials

Directions: Read an editorial and highlight the writer's opinions. Answer the question, and then complete the chart. List the opinions found in the editorial. Do you agree or disagree with the writer's opinion? Then tell how you knew that these statements were opinions.

What is the issue addressed in the editorial? _____

Opinion	Agree or Disagree	How Do You Know?

Name: _____ Date: _____

Station Five: Recognizing Facts

Directions: Read a newspaper article. Write the headline and several fact statements found in the article in the graphic organizer below.

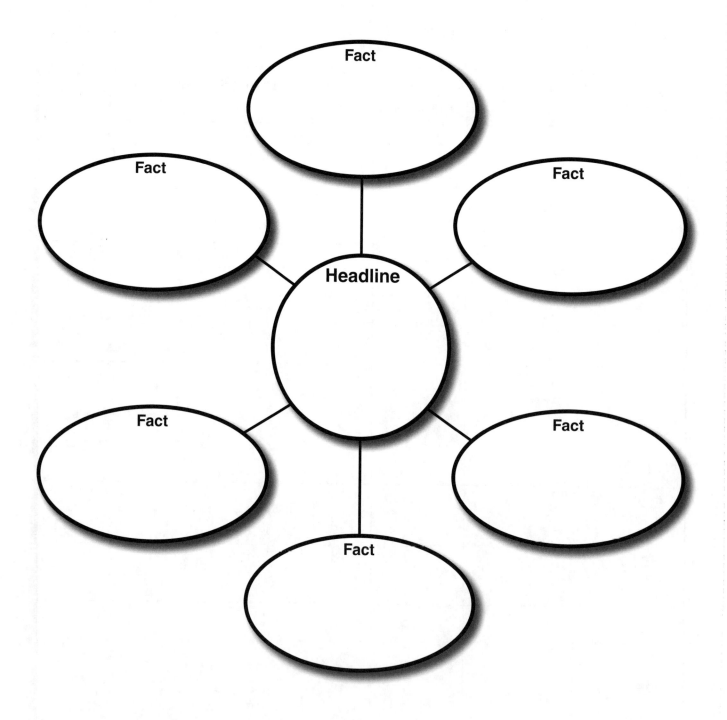

Name: _____ Date: _____

Station Six: Write a Letter to the Editor

Directions: Write a letter to the editor of the school newspaper expressing your opinion about one of the following topics. Give reasons or evidence supporting your opinion.

School Uniforms   In-School Suspension
Year-Round School   Bullying
School Lunches   Extracurricular Activities

Dear Editor:

_____

_____

_____

_____

_____

_____

_____

_____

_____

_____

_____

_____

_____

_____

_____

                                                    Sincerely,

                                          _____
                                                    (Signature)

Handout: Comparing Advertisements

Advertisement #1

Advertisement #2

Teacher Page

Unit: Narrative Techniques: Dialogue

Goal: Students will be able to write, edit, and analyze dialogue.

Common Core State Standards (CCSS):

6th Grade	7th Grade	8th Grade
W.6.3b. Use narrative techniques, such as dialogue, pacing, and description, to develop experiences, events, and/or characters.	W.7.3b. Use narrative techniques, such as dialogue, pacing, and description, to develop experiences, events, and/or characters.	W.8.3b. Use narrative techniques, such as dialogue, pacing, description, and reflection, to develop experiences, events, and/or characters.

© Copyright 2010. National Governors Association Center for Best Practices and Council of Chief State School Officers. All rights reserved.

Materials List/Setup

Station 1: Proofreading Dialogue (Activity); Proofreading Symbols (Handout)
Station 2: Punctuating Dialogue (Activity); Guidelines for Writing Dialogue (Handout)
Station 3: Writing Conversation (Activity); Guidelines for Writing Dialogue (Handout)
Station 4: Analyzing Dialogue (Activity)

Activity: one copy per student
Handout: one copy per each student in a group

Opening: Discussion Questions (Teacher-Directed)

1. What is dialogue?
2. Why do authors use dialogue? (possible answers: develops a character, reveals plot, moves the story along)

Student Instructions for Learning Stations

At the learning stations, you will analyze and write dialogue. Discuss your answer with other team members after completing each activity.

Closure: Reflection

The following questions can be used to stimulate discussion or as a journaling activity.

1. What is the difference between writing dialogue for a story and writing dialogue for a play?
2. How does an author use dialogue to develop a story?

Name: _____ Date: _____

Station One: Proofreading Dialogue

Directions: Use proofreading symbols to mark the errors in capitalization and punctuation found in the passage below.

The harbor master spoke to Ivan and Anna as they watched the restless waters.

"Where are you going, children."

To America, answered Ivan.

"A long way. Three ships bound for america went down last month.

"Ours will not sink" said Ivan.

"Why"

"Because I know it will not"

The harbor master looked at the strange blue eyes of the giant and spoke softly. "you have the eyes of a man who sees things, he said. There was a Norwegian sailor on the *White Queen* with eyes like yours, and he could see death."

"I see life!" said Ivan boldly. "A free life—"

"Hush!" said the harbor master. "Do not speak so loud." He walked swiftly away, but he dropped a ruble into Anna's hand as he passed her by. "For luck" he murmured. "may the little saints look after you on the big waters"

They boarded the ship, and the dream gave them a courage that surprised them. There were others going aboard, and Ivan and Anna felt that those others were also persons who possessed dreams. She saw the dreams in their eyes.

(Excerpt from, "The Citizen" by James Francis Dwyer)

Name: _____   Date: _____

Station Two: Punctuating Dialogue

Directions: Rewrite the sentences below containing dialogue. Add punctuation and capitalization where it is needed. Use the Guidelines for Writing Dialogue handout to help you.

1. Andrew Johnson was the 17th President of the United States said the teacher

   _____

   _____

2. The school nurse explained low calcium levels can increase the likelihood of broken bones

   _____

   _____

3. I learned answered Joyce some insects can walk on the surface of the water

   _____

   _____

4. Alex questioned why is Pluto no longer considered a planet

   _____

   _____

5. what a beautiful day she cried

   _____

   _____

6. Yesterday he interrupted I was not in math class

   _____

   _____

7. I was absent on Wednesday explained Karen

   _____

   _____

Name: _____ Date: _____

Station Three: Writing Conversation

Directions: Write a conversation between two students discussing the new school policy banning all cell phone usage during school hours. Use the Guidelines for Writing Dialogue handout to help you.

_____

_____

_____

_____

_____

_____

_____

_____

_____

_____

_____

_____

_____

_____

_____

_____

_____

_____

_____

_____

Name: _____ Date: _____

Station Four: Analyzing Dialogue

Directions: Dialogue or conversation between characters is often used by the writer to develop the plot, characters, point of view, and theme of a story. Read the dialogue below and answer the following questions.

Ben: Hello, Tom, you got to work?

Tom: (Acting surprised) Why, it's you, Ben! I didn't notice.

Ben: (Taunting) I'm going swimming. Don't you wish you could? But of course you'd rather—WORK.

Tom: What do you call work?

Ben: Why, isn't painting that fence work?

Tom: (Shrugs) Maybe it is, and maybe it ain't.

Ben: Oh come now, you don't mean to let on that you LIKE it?

Tom: (Continues to paint fence) Like it? Well, I don't see why I shouldn't like it. A boy doesn't get a chance to paint a fence every day.

Ben: (Stops eating the apple and watches Tom with interest) Say, Tom, let ME paint a little.

Tom: (Considers) No, no, it wouldn't be right, Ben.

Ben: (Begging) Oh come, now—lemme just try. I'd let you, if it was me. I'll give you my apple.

Tom: (Reluctantly) Here's the brush, Ben. (Ben paints. Tom smirks and munches the apple.)

(play adapted from *The Adventures of Tom Sawyer* by Mark Twain)

---

1. What does the dialogue tell you about the two characters in the play? Cite textual evidence.

   _____

   _____

   _____

"Well, my dear," she said, "how do you like him?"

"He is exactly what John said," he replied; "a pleasanter creature I never wish to mount. What shall we call him?"

"Would you like Ebony?" said she. "He is as black as ebony."

"No, not Ebony."

"Will you call him Blackbird, like your uncle's old horse?"

"No, he is far handsomer than old Blackbird ever was."

"Yes," she said, "he is really quite a beauty, and he has such a sweet, good-tempered face, and such a fine, intelligent eye—what do you say to calling him Black Beauty?"

"Black Beauty—why, yes, I think that is a very good name. If you like it shall be his name;" and so it was.

Excerpt from *Black Beauty* by Anna Sewell

---

2. Why was the horse named Black Beauty? Cite textual evidence.

   _____

   _____

   _____

Handout: Proofreading Symbols

Symbol	Explanation of the Symbol	Example
≡	Capitalize	president Abraham Lincoln
/	Lowercase	fun in the Summer sun
∧	Add a word, letter, or punctuation	Dinosaurs big animals. August 14 2013
∜	Add apostrophe or quotation marks	the queens guard
( )	Delete space	Some one will mail the letter.
⸋	Delete	Respect the the property of others.
sp.	Spelling error	It will be too hours before lunch.
∼	Transpose words or letters	Three pies for dinner Mother baked
↑	Indent	↑Mary and Tom were working on their science fair project.
⊙ ? !	Add a period, question mark, or exclamation mark	My dad fixed spaghetti for dinner
⌗	Begin a new paragraph	⌗The horse's head was too big.
∧#	Add a space	He broke the glass vase.

Handout: Guidelines for Writing Dialogue

1. Dialogue is written or spoken conversation. The exact words of a speaker are called direct quotations. When writing conversation, the exact words of a speaker are enclosed in quotation marks (" ").

Guideline	Example
Begin the quotation with a capital letter.	"**T**he sun emits ultraviolet radiation," explained the teacher.
Place quotation marks before and after a speaker's exact words.	"Turn in your test papers," said Mr. Jones.
Place ending punctuation marks after a speaker's exact words and before the ending quotation mark.	"Can you help me**?**" asked the student.

2. There are two parts to written conversation: the words actually spoken and the tag. The tag identifies who is speaking. Conversation is separated from the tag with a comma, question mark, or exclamation mark. The tag is located before the words spoken, after the words spoken, or interrupts the words spoken.

Separating Conversation From the Tag How to punctuate when the tag . . .	Example
is located after the words spoken.	"We will set up our tents by the river," **explained Josh**.
is located before the words spoken.	**Joyce yelled**, "I won!"
interrupts the words spoken.	"Do you understand," **questioned Mr. Gray**, "that the problem needs more work?"

3. Each time a person speaks, begin a new paragraph.

Example:

> Mariah stared at the flower pots in surprise. The plants had turned brown and lost most of their leaves. "I think we should have watered our plants more often," she said.
> "What are we going to do?" asked Stan. "Our science project is due tomorrow, and all we have to show for weeks of hard work is six dead petunia plants."

Teacher Page

Unit: Editing and Proofreading

Goal: Students will be able to incorporate editing and proofreading skills in their writing.

Common Core State Standards (CCSS):

6th Grade	7th Grade	8th Grade
W.6.5. With some guidance and support from peers and adults, develop and strengthen writing as needed by planning, revising, editing, rewriting, or trying a new approach.	W.7.5. With some guidance and support from peers and adults, develop and strengthen writing as needed by planning, revising, editing, rewriting, or trying a new approach, focusing on how well purpose and audience have been addressed.	W.8.5. With some guidance and support from peers and adults, develop and strengthen writing as needed by planning, revising, editing, rewriting, or trying a new approach, focusing on how well purpose and audience have been addressed.

© Copyright 2010. National Governors Association Center for Best Practices and Council of Chief State School Officers. All rights reserved.

Materials List/Setup

Station 1: Proofreading a Business Letter (Activity); Proofreading Symbols* (Handout)
Station 2: Punctuation, Capitalization and Grammar (Activity); Proofreading Symbols* (Handout)
Station 3: Editing for Clarity, Transition, and Order (Activity); Proofreading Symbols* (Handout)
Station 4: Proofreading Scavenger Hunt (Activity); Proofreading Symbols* (Handout)

Activity Pages: one copy per student
Handout: Proofreading Symbols—one copy per each student in a group

* Note: The handout is located in the unit "Narrative Techniques: Dialogue (page 16)."

Opening: Discussion Questions (Teacher-Directed)

1. What is the difference between editing and proofreading?
2. Why is it helpful to have someone proofread your writing?

Student Instructions for Learning Stations

At the learning stations, you will practice your editing and proofreading skills. Discuss your answers with other team members after completing each activity.

Closure: Reflection

The following questions can be used to stimulate discussion or as a journaling activity.

1. Why is it important to edit your work before proofreading?
2. How do editing and proofreading help a writer improve his or her work?

Name: _____   Date: _____

Station One: Proofreading a Business Letter

Directions: Proofread and correct the following business letter using proofreading marks.

1031 south Market

Mt Vernon, Illinois 77089

Feburary 19 2013

Kathryn Brown

National Park Service

U.S. Department of the Interior

Washington DC 20025

Dear Ms. Brown:

In Social Studies class I am doing a research project on wolfes in the Yellowstone National park. I am having trouble finding up-to-date information on the reintroduction of wolves to the Park and the effect it had has on the buffalo population. please send me any free booklets or fact sheets on the wolf population.. I would appriciate the addresses of any websites that would help me with my research.

Thank you very much for your help

Sincerly,

Ann Reynolds

Why is it important to edit and proofread a business letter before sending it?

_____

_____

_____

Name: _____ Date: _____

Station Two: Punctuation, Capitalization, and Grammar

Directions: Proofread and correct each passage using proofreading marks.

Punctuation Passage

Did you know Margaret Corbin was one of the first women to receive a military pension for her service during the American Revolution. During the Battle of Fort Washington in 1776 Margaret Corbin did more than cook for the men of the regiment She also stood by her husbands side at the cannon to hand him ammunition. When he was killed in battle she took his place. She loaded and fired the cannon until she was severely wounded. After the battle soldiers took her across the Hudson River to Fort Lee New Jersey, where she received medical care.

(From *Reading Tutor: Biographies* by Maureen Betz. Used with permission of Mark Twain Media, Inc., Publishers)

Capitalization Passage

When you visit the statue of Liberty at the entrance to New York Harbor, be sure to stop at the pedestal. You will find lines from a poem called "the New Colossus."

Emma Lazarus wrote these words. She was an american poet who composed the sonnet in 1883 to raise money for the statue of Liberty's Pedestal.

In 1903, the last five lines were carved into the base of the statue of Liberty to welcome the millions of Immigrants entering the United states.

(From *Reading Tutor: Biographies* by Maureen Betz. Used with permission of Mark Twain Media, Inc., Publishers)

Grammar Passage

A judge's powers and responsibilities is impressive. But how do a person become a judge? There is four methods for selecting a judge. The first is through popular election; citizens use the ballot box to vote for their favorite candidate. The candidate who receives the mostest votes wins the position of judge.

(From *Democracy, Law, and Justice* by Daniel S.Campagna and Ann Beauchamp Campagna. Used with permission of Mark Twain Media, Inc., Publishers)

Name: _____   Date: _____

Station Three: Editing for Clarity, Transition, and Order

Editing involves checking word order, transitions, wordiness, and sentence variety to make sure the writing flows more effectively.

Directions: Using proofreading symbols, edit the sentences below according to the directions given for each. Write the sentences correctly on the lines provided.

1. **Combine the two sentences using a transition word.**

   My dog is spoiled. He only eats table scraps.

   _____

   _____

2. **Change the order of the words in the sentence.**

   Destroyed by the tornado, the family looked at the remains of their home.

   _____

   _____

3. **Delete extra words and change the word order in the sentence.**

   The president spoke to the audience; he spoke with great conviction.

   _____

   _____

4. **Delete the unnecessary words in the sentence.**

   Good cooks follow the recipe and gather the ingredients and follow the directions step by step.

   _____

   _____

5. **Change word order in the sentence to make the meaning clearer.**

   Spectators began to arrive at Cape Canaveral Tuesday morning.

   _____

   _____

6. **Combine two sentences with a conjunction.**

   The hometown team scored a touchdown. The spectators cheered loudly.

   _____

   _____

Name: _____ Date: _____

Station Four: Proofreading Scavenger Hunt

Directions: Locate the 21 errors in grammar, punctuation, spelling, and capitalization in the passage below. Mark the errors using the proper proofreading symbols.

The Day the Mississippi Ran Backwards

Few people are aware that in 1811 the larges series of earthquakes to hit north America occurred in New Madrid Missouri. New Madrid was a town located in the southeast corner of the state on the Mississippi river. In the early part of the nineteenth century it was a prosperous community and considered an important landing between the Ohio River and Natchez Mississippi. The people living in New Madrid were well aware of the dangers of living close to the river. Spring floods were a recurring part of life in New Madrid.

But, as the citizens of New Madrid went to bed on the evening of December 15, 1811 they were about to learn of another danger of living in this area. At a little after 2 am., a low rumbling began and grew in intensity. Dishs fell from tables and cabinets. Furniture crashed to the floor Chimneys collapsed. Cabins and homes began to creek and groan with such intensity, the residents ran outside before their homes were destroyed. This was the first of several major shocks to hit the region through out the winter. People talked about the New Madrid earthquake, but actually there were several major quakes and thousands of aftershocks that occurred through the Winter of 1811–1812. It has been estimated that these quakes ranked between 8.0 and 8.5 on the Richter scale.

People who lived through the quakes and wrote about what they see have left a vivid description of the awesome power of this natural disaster. these descriptions tell us that the earth actualy rolled in waves, as if it were a lake and not land. Deep crevasses appeared and swallowed trees, horses, and cows. Long fissures, several hundred feet long, belched a foul sulphur odor and spewed out sand water, and mud.

Those who was on the Mississippi during the quakes had even more bizarre and terrifying storys. To some, it appeared as if the river sprang to life. Huge waves rocked and swamped boats. The water boiled and swirled. Fissures opened under neath the surface and caused whirlpools. Debris shot through the surface, as if shot from a cannon. In some spots, the river dropped several feet, and falls were formed. Banks toppled into the river. Lakes were created. It has been reported that the river was in such an agitated state, that for several hours, it ran backwards

(From *Disasters* by Don Blattner and Lisa Howerton. Used with permission of Mark Twain Media, Inc., Publishers)

Teacher Page

Unit: Analyzing and Drawing Evidence From Informational Text

Goal: Students will be able to analyze photographs on a central theme and make inferences on the details.

Common Core State Standards (CCSS):

6th Grade	7th Grade	8th Grade
W.6.9. Draw evidence from literary or informational texts to support analysis, reflection, and research.	W.7.9. Draw evidence from literary or informational texts to support analysis, reflection, and research.	W.8.9. Draw evidence from literary or informational texts to support analysis, reflection, and research.

© Copyright 2010. National Governors Association Center for Best Practices and Council of Chief State School Officers. All rights reserved.

Materials List/Setup

Station 1: Details! Details! Details (Activity); Textile Mill Workers: Photograph A (Activity)
Station 2: Details! Details! Details (Activity); Textile Mill Workers: Photograph B (Activity)
Station 3: Details! Details! Details (Activity); Textile Mill Workers: Photograph C (Activity)
Station 4: Details! Details! Details (Activity); Textile Mill Workers: Photograph D (Activity)
Station 5: Details! Details! Details (Activity); Textile Mill Workers: Photograph E (Activity)
Station 6: Details! Details! Details (Activity); Textile Mill Workers: Photograph F (Activity)

Activity: Details! Details! Details!—one copy per student for each station
        Textile Mill Workers: Photographs A–F—one copy per each student in a group

*Integration of Technology Skills—For additional pictures go online to <http://www.loc.gov/index.html>. Access the Print and Photographs Collection. Conduct a keyword search on textile mill workers.

Opening: Discussion Questions (Teacher-Directed)

1. Do you have old photograph albums at home that contain pictures of unidentified people?
2. Are there clues within a photograph that can help you identify the people, place, time, or purpose for it being taken?
3. Can you draw inferences from the clues?

Student Instructions for Learning Stations

At each station, examine the photograph of textile mill workers from the early 1900s and make inferences about your observations. Look at the body language, facial expressions, clothing, and age of the workers. Study the setting of the pictures. Observe any actions of the people or objects. Look closely for any textual clues that appear within the picture. From your observations, you will make inferences about textile mill workers and the jobs they performed. Discuss your answers with other team members after completing each activity.

Closure: Reflection

Students will use the completed learning station activities to help compose the Reflection: Textile Mill Workers writing activity.

Name: _____ Date: _____

Activity: Details! Details! Details!

Photograph: A   B   C   D   E   F   (Circle the letter of the photograph for this station.)

Directions: Examine the photograph closely. Begin by looking at the photograph as a whole; then focus on the individual details. Fill in the chart below.

Detail (What I Observe)	This leads me to question…	Inference (My Best Guess)

Station One: Textile Mill Workers: Photograph A

Photo by: Lewis Wickes Hine, Nov. 1908. Library of Congress <http://hdl.loc.gov/loc.pnp/nclc.01350>

Station Two: Textile Mill Workers: Photograph B

Photo by: Lewis Wickes Hine, Dec. 1908. Library of Congress <http://hdl.loc.gov/loc.pnp/nclc.01476>

Station Three: Textile Mill Workers: Photograph C

Photo by: Lewis Wickes Hine, Nov. 1908. Library of Congress <http://hdl.loc.gov/loc.pnp/nclc.01383>

Station Four: Textile Mill Workers: Photograph D

Photo by: Lewis Wickes Hine, Nov. 1908. Library of Congress <http://hdl.loc.gov/loc.pnp/nclc.01362>

Station Five: Textile Mill Workers: Photograph E

Photo by: Lewis Wickes Hine, Nov. 1908. Library of Congress <http://hdl.loc.gov/loc.pnp/nclc.01357>

Station Six: Textile Mill Workers: Photograph F

Photo by: Lewis Wickes Hine, Jan. 1909. Library of Congress <http://hdl.loc.gov/loc.pnp/nclc.01583>

Name: _____ Date: _____

Reflection: Textile Mill Workers

Directions: From the photographs you have observed, what inferences can you make about textile mill workers in the early 1900s and the jobs they performed? Cite evidence from the photographs to support your answer.

_____

_____

_____

_____

_____

_____

_____

_____

_____

_____

_____

_____

_____

_____

_____

_____

_____

_____

Teacher Page

Unit: Analyzing and Drawing Evidence From Literature

Goal: Students will be able to draw evidence from and analyze character types and patterns of events from a traditional story and the modern variations of the same title. Students will also be able to compare and contrast a traditional story and a modern variation of the story in poetry form.

Common Core State Standards (CCSS):

6th Grade	7th Grade	8th Grade
W.6.9. Draw evidence from literary or informational texts to support analysis, reflection, and research.	W.7.9. Draw evidence from literary or informational texts to support analysis, reflection, and research.	W.8.9. Draw evidence from literary or informational texts to support analysis, reflection, and research.

© Copyright 2010. National Governors Association Center for Best Practices and Council of Chief State School Officers. All rights reserved.

Materials List/Setup

Station 1: Character Traits (Activity); Book: *The Three Horrid Little Pigs* by Liz Pichon
Station 2: Flat or Round Characters (Activity)
Station 3: Static and Dynamic Characters (Activity); Assortment of Books [Note to Teacher—See: *The Three Little Pigs* (Modern Variations) Teacher Resource Page for a list of titles.]
Station 4: Story Map (Activity); Protagonist or Antagonist (Activity); Book: *The Three Little Wolves and the Big Bad Pig* by Eugene Trivizas
Station 5: *The Three Little Pigs:* Story and Poem (Activity); Copy of the poem "The Three Little Pigs" from the book *Revolting Rhymes* by Roald Dahl

Activity Pages: one copy per student per station
Handouts: One copy per student of Examples of Character Traits and *The Three Little Pigs* (Trad. Ver.).
Books: Either every student in a group will need one book, one student in the group could read the book to the entire group, or the students can take turns reading the book. (Integration of Speaking and Listening Skills)

*Integration of Technology Skills—Students could watch online a visual interpretation of "The Three Little Pigs" from the book *Revolting Rhymes* at <http://www.youtube.com/watch?v=F5DS2DnsJ04>.

Opening: Discussion Questions (Teacher-Directed)

1. What are some character types? (possible answers: round, flat, static, dynamic, protagonist, antagonist)
2. What are character traits? (Note to teacher: see Examples of Character Traits handout)
3. How does an author reveal character traits of a character? (possible answers: actions, author's words, thoughts, emotions)

Student Instructions for Learning Stations

At the learning stations, examine, draw evidence from, and analyze character types and patterns of events from the traditional story of *The Three Little Pigs* and the modern variations of this story. Also, compare and contrast the traditional story with a modern variation of the story in poetry form. Discuss your answers with other team members after completing each activity.

Closure: Reflection

Students will use their completed learning station activities to help compose the Reflection: Traditional Versus Modern Variations writing activity.

Name: _____   Date: _____

Station One: Character Traits

Directions: Character traits are how a character acts, feels, looks, and speaks. In the appropriate graphic organizer below, list the character traits of the wolf in the traditional story and the character traits of the wolf in the book *The Three Horrid Little Pigs* by Liz Pichon. Use textual evidence to support your answers.

The Three Little Pigs (Traditional Version)

Wolf's Character Traits	Textual Evidence

The Three Horrid Little Pigs by Liz Pichon (Modern Variation)

Wolf's Character Traits	Textual Evidence

How do the character traits of the wolf in the traditional story compare to the character traits of the wolf in the modern variation? Explain your answer.

_____

_____

_____

_____

Name: _____   Date: _____

Station Two: Flat or Round Characters

In a story, a round character is well-developed. It is easy to identify their personality and physical and emotional traits. A flat character is the opposite of a round character. This type of character is not well-developed and seems to be one-dimensional.

Directions: Review the traditional version of *The Three Little Pigs*. Determine if the characters are flat or round. Cite textual evidence to support your decision.

Character	Flat or Round?
Wolf	Is the character flat or round?
	Cite textual evidence:
First Little Pig	Is the character flat or round?
	Cite textual evidence:
Second Little Pig	Is the character flat or round?
	Cite textual evidence:
Third Little Pig	Is the character flat or round?
	Cite textual evidence:

Name: _____ Date: _____

Station Three: Static and Dynamic Characters

During a story, a static character does not change or evolve. The dynamic character will undergo a change, usually brought about by the resolution of a conflict or the result of having faced a crisis.

Directions: Read a modern variation of *The Three Little Pigs*. From the book, select one of the major characters and complete the character development graphic organizer. Cite textual evidence to support your findings.

Title of the Book: _____

Character: _____

Character Development

Beginning

Major Character Traits

Actions

Ending

Major Character Traits

Actions

1. Did a crisis or event cause the character to change? Explain your answer.

   _____

   _____

2. Is the character static or dynamic? Use textual evidence to support your answer.

   _____

   _____

Name: _____ Date: _____

Station Four: Story Map

Directions: Complete the story map for the traditional version of *The Three Little Pigs* and its modern variation, *The Three Little Wolves and the Big Bad Pig* by Eugene Trivizas.

The Three Little Pigs	*The Three Little Wolves and the Big Bad Pig*
Theme	
Setting	
Characters	
Conflict	
Pattern of Major Events	
Conclusion	

Name: _____ Date: _____

Station Four: Protagonist or Antagonist

The **protagonist** is usually the hero of the story. He or she resolves the conflict created by the **antagonist**, or the villain. A story map can help you to identify the protagonist and antagonist.

Directions: Analyze your completed story map to identify the protagonist and antagonist in each story. Use details from the story map to support your answer.

1. *The Three Little Pigs* (Traditional)

Protagonist: _____

_____

_____

_____

Antagonist: _____

_____

_____

_____

2. *The Three Little Wolves and the Big Bad Pig* by Eugene Trivizas

Protagonist: _____

_____

_____

_____

Antagonist: _____

_____

_____

_____

Name: _____ Date: _____

Station Five: *The Three Little Pigs: Story and Poem*

Directions: Compare and contrast the events in the traditional story version of *The Three Little Pigs* to the events in the poem, "The Three Pigs" by Roald Dahl.

Story	Both	Poem

Name: _____ Date: _____

Reflection: Traditional Versus Modern Variations

Directions: Describe how the theme, setting, characters, conflict, pattern of events, and conclusion in one of the modern variations differs from the traditional version of *The Three Little Pigs.* Cite textual evidence to support your answer.

_____

_____

_____

_____

_____

_____

_____

_____

_____

_____

_____

_____

_____

_____

_____

_____

_____

_____

Handout: *The Three Little Pigs* (Traditional Version)

Once upon a time there was an old Sow with three little Pigs, and as she had not enough to keep them, she sent them out to seek their fortune.

The first that went off met a Man with a bundle of straw, and said to him, "Please, Man, give me that straw to build me a house"; which the Man did, and the little Pig built a house with it. Presently came along a Wolf, and knocked at the door, and said, "Little Pig, little Pig, let me come in."

To which the Pig answered, "No, no, by the hair of my chinny chin chin."

"Then I'll huff and I'll puff, and I'll blow your house in!" said the Wolf. So he huffed and he puffed, and he blew his house in, and ate up the little Pig.

The second Pig met a Man with a bundle of furze [sticks], and said, "Please, Man, give me that furze to build a house"; which the Man did, and the Pig built his house.

Then along came the Wolf and said, "Little Pig, little Pig, let me come in."

"No, no, by the hair of my chinny chin chin."

"Then I'll puff and I'll huff, and I'll blow your house in!" So he huffed and he puffed, and he puffed and he huffed, and at last he blew the house down, and ate up the second little Pig.

The third little Pig met a Man with a load of bricks, and said, "Please, Man, give me those bricks to build a house with"; so the Man gave him the bricks, and he built his house with them. So the Wolf came, as he did to the other little Pigs, and said, "Little Pig, little Pig, let me come in."

"No, no, by the hair of my chinny chin chin."

"Then I'll huff and I'll puff, and I'll blow your house in."

Well, he huffed and he puffed, and he huffed and he puffed, and he puffed and he huffed; but he could not get the house down. When he found that he could not, with all his huffing and puffing, blow the house down, he said, "Little Pig, I know where there is a nice field of turnips."

"Where?" said the little Pig.

"Oh, in Mr. Smith's home-field; and if you will be ready to-morrow morning, I will call for you, and we will go together and get some for dinner."

"Very well," said the little Pig, "I will be ready. What time do you mean to go?"

"Oh, at six o'clock."

Well, the little Pig got up at five, and got the turnips and was home again before six. When the Wolf came he said, "Little Pig, are you ready?"

"Ready!" said the little Pig, "I have been and come back again, and got a nice pot-full for dinner."

Handout: *The Three Little Pigs* (cont.)

The Wolf felt very angry at this, but thought that he would be up to the little Pig somehow or other; so he said, "Little Pig, I know where there is a nice apple-tree."

"Where?" said the Pig.

"Down at Merry-garden," replied the Wolf; "and if you will not deceive me, I will come for you at five o'clock to-morrow, and we will go together and get some apples."

Well, the little Pig woke at four the next morning, and bustled up, and went off for the apples, hoping to get back before the Wolf came; but he had farther to go, and had to climb the tree, so that just as he was coming down from it, he saw the Wolf coming, which, as you may suppose, frightened him very much. When the Wolf came up, he said, "Little Pig, what! are you here before me? Are they nice apples?"

"Yes, very," said the little Pig; "I will throw you down one." And he threw it so far that, while the Wolf was gone to pick it up, the little Pig jumped down and ran home.

The next day the Wolf came again, and said to the little Pig, "Little Pig, there is a Fair in the Town this afternoon: will you go?"

"Oh, yes," said the Pig, "I will go; what time shall you be ready?"

"At three," said the Wolf.

So the little Pig went off before the time, as usual, and got to the Fair, and bought a butter churn, and was on his way home with it when he saw the Wolf coming. Then he could not tell what to do. So he got into the churn to hide, and in doing so turned it round, and it began to roll, and rolled down the hill with the Pig inside it, which frightened the Wolf so much that he ran home without going to the Fair.

He went to the little Pig's house, and told him how frightened he had been by a great round thing which came down the hill past him.

Then the little Pig said, "Hah! I frightened you, did I? I had been to the Fair and bought a butter churn, and when I saw you I got into it, and rolled down the hill."

Then the Wolf was very angry indeed, and declared he would eat up the little Pig, and that he would get down the chimney after him.

When the little Pig saw what he was about, he hung on the pot full of water, and made up a blazing fire, and, just as the Wolf was coming down, took off the cover of the pot, and in fell the Wolf. And the little Pig put on the cover again in an instant, boiled him up, and ate him for supper, and lived happily ever after.

(*The Story of the Three Little Pigs.* drawings by L. Leslie Brooke. New York: Frederick Warne & Company, 1904.)

Handout: Examples of Character Traits

adaptable	determined	immature	proud
adventurous	discouraged	impatient	rash
affectionate	dishonest	impulsive	reliable
afraid	disrespectful	incompetent	reserved
aggressive	dominant	indecisive	respectful
ambitious	dreamer	independent	responsible
angry	eager	influencial	romantic
annoyed	easy-going	insecure	rude
apologetic	eloquent	intelligent	ruthless
argumentative	embarrassed	inventive	sarcastic
arrogant	encouraging	irritable	scared
awkward	energetic	jealous	secretive
bored	expert	jovial	self-centered
bossy	faithful	lazy	selfish
brave	fearless	leader	sensitive
calm	fidgety	light-hearted	serious
capable	fierce	logical	shrewd
careless	flamboyant	lonely	shy
cautious	flexible	lovable	silly
charming	foolish	loyal	sly
cheerful	friendly	malicious	smart
clever	frustrated	mean	sneaky
cold-hearted	funny	meek	spoiled
commanding	furious	mischievous	squeamish
compassionate	generous	mysterious	stingy
compulsive	gentle	nagging	strong
conceited	giving	naïve	stubborn
concerned	glamorous	nervous	studious
confident	gloomy	obedient	successful
confused	grateful	obnoxious	sympathetic
considerate	greedy	observant	talented
consistent	grouchy	optimistic	thankful
controlling	gullible	patient	thoughtful
cooperative	happy	patriotic	thrifty
courageous	hard-working	perceptive	timid
cowardly	hateful	persevering	trusting
crafty	helpful	persistent	trustworthy
creative	hesitant	persuasive	unfriendly
cruel	honest	picky	unhappy
curious	hopeful	polite	wise
demanding	hospitable	popular	witty
dependable	humble	practical	

Teacher Resource Page: *The Three Little Pigs*
(Modern Variations)

Artell, Mike. *Three Little Cajun Pigs*, 2003.

Asch, Frank. *Ziggy Piggy and the Three Little Pigs*, 1998.

Dahl, Roald. *Revolting Rhymes*, 1982.

Delessert, Etienne. *Big and Bad*, 2008.

Geist, Ken. *The Three Little Fish and the Big Bad Shark*, 2007.

Guarnaccia, Steven. *The Three Little Pigs: An Architectural Tale*, 2010.

Harris, Jim. *The Three Little Dinosaurs*, 1999.

Kellogg, Steven. *The Three Little Pigs*, 1997.

Ketteman, Helen. *The Three Little Gators*, 2009.

Laverde, Arlene. *Alaska's Three Pigs*, 2000.

Lowell, Susan. *The Three Little Javelinas*, 1992.

Marshall, James. *The Three Little Pigs*, 1989.

Moser, Barry. *The Three Little Pigs*, 2001.

Pichon, Liz. *The Three Horrid Little Pigs*, 2008.

Ross, Tony. *The Three Pigs*, 1983.

Scieszka, Jon. *The True Story of the 3 Little Pigs: By A. Wolf*, 1989.

Trivizas, Eugene. *The Three Little Wolves and the Big Bad Pig*, 1993.

Trumbauer, Lisa. *The Three Little Pigs: The Graphic Novel*, 2009.

Walton, Rick. *Pig Pigger Piggest*, 1997.

Whatley, Bruce. *Wait! No Paint!*, 2001.

Wiesner, David. *The Three Pigs*, 2001.

Answer Keys

*If applicable, answers were provided.

Unit: Fact and Opinion
Fact and Opinion in Advertising (p. 6)
Advertisement #1
Claim: Motorists love to read billboards!
Facts: low-cost advertising
Opinions: best way to reach new customers
Advertisement #2
Claim: Proposition B is the best way to make our highways safe.
Facts: distract drivers; advertise controversial subjects
Opinions: block the beautiful scenery
1. Answers may vary.
2. Answers may vary.

Unit: Narrative Techniques: Dialogue
Proofreading Dialogue (p. 12)

> The harbor master spoke to Ivan and Anna as they watched the restless waters.
> "Where are you going, children?"
> "To America," answered Ivan.
> "A long way. Three ships bound for america went down last month."
> "Ours will not sink," said Ivan.
> "Why?"
> "Because I know it will not."
> The harbor master looked at the strange blue eyes of the giant and spoke softly. "you have the eyes of a man who sees things," he said. "There was a Norwegian sailor on the *White Queen* with eyes like yours, and he could see death."
> "I see life!" said Ivan boldly. "A free life—"
> "Hush!" said the harbor master. "Do not speak so loud." He walked swiftly away, but he dropped a ruble into Anna's hand as he passed her by. "For luck," he murmured. "may the little saints look after you on the big waters."
> They boarded the ship, and the dream gave them a courage that surprised them. There were others going aboard, and Ivan and Anna felt that those others were also persons who possessed dreams. She saw the dreams in their eyes.
>
> (Excerpt from, "The Citizen" by James Francis Dwyer)

Punctuating Dialogue (p. 13)
1. "Andrew Johnson was the 17th President of the United States," said the teacher.
2. The school nurse explained, "Low calcium levels can increase the likelihood of broken bones."
3. "I learned," answered Joyce, "some insects can walk on the surface of the water."
4. Alex questioned, "Why is Pluto no longer considered a planet?"
5. "What a beautiful day!" she cried.
6. "Yesterday," he interrupted, "I was not in math class."
7. "I was absent on Wednesday," explained Karen.

Analyzing Dialogue (p. 15)
1. The words "Tom smirks and munches the apple" reveals Tom's mischievous nature. You can tell he was trying to trick Ben into painting the fence for him. The words "I'll give you my apple" shows that Ben was gullible and fell for Tom's trick.
2. The two phrases "He is as black as ebony" and "he is really quite a beauty" explain why the horse was named Black Beauty.

Unit: Editing and Proofreading
Proofreading a Business Letter (p. 19)

> 1031 south Market
> Mt Vernon, Illinois 77089
> February 19 2013
>
>
> Kathryn Brown
> National Park Service
> U.S. Department of the Interior
> Washington DC 20025
>
> Dear Ms. Brown:
>
> In Social Studies class I am doing a research project on wolfes in the Yellowstone National park. I am having trouble finding up-to-date information on the reintroduction of wolves to the Park and the effect it had has on the buffalo population. please send me any free booklets or fact sheets on the wolf population. I would appriciate the addresses of any Websites that would help me with my research.
>
> Thank you very much for your help.
>
> Sincerly,
>
> Ann Reynolds

Punctuation, Capitalization, and Grammar (p. 20)

> **Punctuation Passage**
>
> Did you know Margaret Corbin was one of the first women to receive a military pension for her service during the American Revolution During the Battle of Fort Washington in 1776 Margaret Corbin did more than cook for the men of the regiment She also stood by her husbands side at the cannon to hand him ammunition. When he was killed in battle she took his place. She loaded and fired the cannon until she was severely wounded. After the battle soldiers took her across the Hudson River to Fort Lee New Jersey, where she received medical care.
>
> (From *Reading Tutor: Biographies* by Maureen Betz. Used with permission of Mark Twain Media, Inc., Publishers)

Capitalization Passage

When you visit the statue of Liberty at the entrance to New York Harbor, be sure to stop at the pedestal. You will find lines from a poem called "the New Colossus."

Emma Lazarus wrote these words. She was an american poet who composed the sonnet in 1883 to raise money for the statue of Liberty's Pedestal.

In 1903, the last five lines were carved into the base of the statue of Liberty to welcome the millions of immigrants entering the United states.

(From Reading Tutor: Biographies by Maureen Betz. Used with permission of Mark Twain Media, Inc., Publishers)

Grammar Passage

A judge's powers and responsibilities are impressive. But how does a person become a judge? There is four methods for selecting a judge. The first is through popular election; citizens use the ballot box to vote for their favorite candidate. The candidate who receives the most votes wins the position of judge.

(From Democracy, Law, and Justice by Daniel S. Campagna and Ann Beauchamp Campagna. Used with permission of Mark Twain Media, Inc., Publishers)

Editing for Clarity, Transition, and Order (p. 21)

1. My dog is spoiled because he only eats table scraps.
2. The family looked at the remains of their home destroyed by the tornado.
3. The president spoke with great conviction to the audience.
4. Good cooks gather the ingredients and follow the directions in the recipe step by step.
5. On Tuesday morning, spectators began to arrive at Cape Canaveral.
6. The hometown team scored a touchdown, and the spectators cheered loudly.

Proofreading Scavenger Hunt (p. 22)

The Day the Mississippi Ran Backwards

Few people are aware that in 1811 the largest series of earthquakes to hit north America occurred in New Madrid, Missouri. New Madrid was a town located in the southeast corner of the state on the Mississippi river. In the early part of the nineteenth century, it was a prosperous community and considered an important landing between the Ohio River and Natchez, Mississippi. The people living in New Madrid were well aware of the dangers of living close to the river. Spring floods were a recurring part of life in New Madrid.

But, as the citizens of New Madrid went to bed on the evening of December 15, 1811, they were about to learn of another danger of living in this area. At a little after 2 am., a low rumbling began and grew in intensity. Dishes fell from tables and cabinets. Furniture crashed to the floor. Chimneys collapsed. Cabins and homes began to creak and groan with such intensity, the residents ran outside before their homes were destroyed. This was the first of several major shocks to hit the region through out the winter. People talked about the New Madrid earthquake, but actually there were several major quakes and thousands of aftershocks that occurred through the Winter of 1811–1812. It has been estimated that these quakes ranked between 8.0 and 8.5 on the Richter scale.

People who lived through the quakes and wrote about what they saw have left a vivid description of the awesome power of this natural disaster. These descriptions tell us that the earth actually rolled in waves, as if it were a lake and not land. Deep crevasses appeared and swallowed trees, horses, and cows. Long fissures, several hundred feet long, belched a foul sulphur odor and spewed out sand, water, and mud.

Those who was on the Mississippi during the quakes had even more bizarre and terrifying storys. To some, it appeared as if the river sprang to life. Huge waves rocked and swamped boats. The water boiled and swirled. Fissures opened underneath the surface and caused whirlpools. Debris shot through the surface, as if shot from a cannon. In some spots, the river dropped several feet, and falls were formed. Banks toppled into the river. Lakes were created. It has been reported that the river was in such an agitated state, that for several hours, it ran backwards.

(From Disasters by Don Blattner and Lisa Howerton. Used with permission of Mark Twain Media, Inc., Publishers)

Unit: Analyzing and Drawing Evidence From Informational Text

The activities for this unit will require teacher verification.

Unit: Analyzing and Drawing Evidence From Literature

Flat or Round Characters (p. 34)

Wolf: Round; Textual evidence will vary.
First Little Pig: Flat; Textual evidence will vary.
Second Little Pig: Flat; Textual evidence will vary.
Third Little Pig: Round; Textual evidence will vary.

Story Map (p. 36)

The Three Little Pigs

Theme: Good versus evil.

Setting: rural area; could be any time period up to modern day

Characters: Wolf; first, second, and third little pigs; Mother Pig; men with straw, furze (sticks), and bricks

Conflict: The big bad wolf wants to eat the three little pigs.

Pattern of Major Events:

1. Mother Sow sends the three little pigs off to seek their fortune.
2. First pig meets a man with a load of straw and builds a straw house.
3. The wolf blows down the straw house and eats the first pig.
4. Second pig meets a man with a load of furze (sticks) and builds a stick house.
5. The wolf blows down the stick house and eats the pig.
6. The third pig meets a man with a load of bricks and builds a brick house. Wolf can't blow down the brick house.
7. Wolf tries to trick the third little pig into coming out of the house for turnips, apples, and to go to the fair. The pig always beats the wolf out and back or outsmarts the wolf.
8. Wolf goes down the chimney and falls into a pot of boiling water.
9. The third little pig eats the wolf.

Conclusion: The wolf falls down the chimney into a pot of boiling water. The pig boils the wolf up and eats him.

The Three Little Wolves and the Big Bad Pig

Theme: Good versus evil.

Setting: long ago

Characters: Big Bad Pig, three little wolves, Mother Wolf, kangaroo, beaver, rhinoceros, and flamingo

Conflict: The Big Bad Pig wanted to come into the houses of the three little wolves.

Pattern of Major Events:

1. Mother Wolf sends the three wolves out into the world.
2. The three wolves meet a kangaroo with a load of bricks and build their house.
3. The pig knocks down the house with a sledge hammer. The wolves escape.
4. The three wolves meet a beaver who has concrete, and they build a concrete house.
5. The pig smashes the house with a pneumatic drill. The wolves escape.
6. The three wolves meet a rhinoceros. They build a very strong house.
7. The pig dynamites this house and blows it up.
8. The three wolves meet a flamingo who gives them flowers. The wolves build a house of flowers.
9. Pig tries to destroy the flower house.
10. The pig smells the flowers.
11. The pig's heart grows tender and he becomes a good pig.
12. The pig moves in with the wolves, and they live happily ever after.

Conclusion: The pig's heart grows tender after smelling the flowers and he becomes a good pig. The pig moves in with the wolves, and they live happily ever after.

Protagonist or Antagonist (p. 37)

1. Protagonist: Third Little Pig; Details will vary.
   Antagonist: Wolf; Details will vary.
2. Protagonist: Wolves; Details will vary.
   Antagonist: Pig; Details will vary.

The Three Little Pigs: **Story and Poem (p. 38)**

Story:

1. The mother sow says goodbye to her little pigs.
2. The third little pig builds his house of bricks.
3. Wolf and the third little pig agree to go get turnips and apples.
4. Wolf and the third little pig agree to go to the fair. The pig escapes in a butter churn.
5. Wolf goes down the chimney and falls into a pot of boiling water.
6. The third little pig eats the wolf for supper.

Both:

1. First little pig builds his house of straw.
2. Wolf blows down the straw house.
3. Second little pig builds his house of furze (sticks).
4. Wolf blows down stick house.
5. Wolf tries to blow down the house of the third little pig.

Poem:

1. First pig begins to pray.
2. The wolf eats the first pig quite fast.
3. Second pig wants to talk and make a deal.
4. Wolf threatens to blow up the third pig's house with dynamite.
5. Third pig calls Red Riding Hood and asks for help.
6. Red Riding Hood comes to help and kills the wolf with a single shot.
7. The third pig congratulates Red Riding Hood.
8. Red Riding Hood kills the third pig and turns his skin into a pigskin traveling case.